It Only Takes a Moment
to Score

It Only Takes a Moment to Score

✦

The Entrepreneur's Guide to Successfully Selling Business Ideas

Robert Moment

iUniverse, Inc.
New York Lincoln Shanghai

It Only Takes a Moment to Score
The Entrepreneur's Guide to Successfully Selling Business Ideas

iUniverse, Inc.

For information address:
iUniverse, Inc.
2021 Pine Lake Road, Suite 100
Lincoln, NE 68512
www.iuniverse.com

This material is provided for informational use only and as means of helping those interested in professional and holistic growth.
Use of this material is the responsibility of the reader.

Additional copies of this book can be ordered through our web site at

www.sellintegrity.com

ISBN: 0-595-31833-9

Printed in the United States of America

This book is dedicated to my beloved parents and my brother
who have provided me with the courage, love and support
so necessary for believing in my ideas, my message
and mostly myself.

Contents

Foreword

As a well-established business strategist for more than two decades, I am often asked to what I attribute the success I have achieved thus far in the business world. Although my response sounds simple, it is always the same. While formal education and sales training have served me well, I have discovered that people enjoy doing business with those they trust. In fact, as my business evolved, I began noticing how the development of trust factored into higher levels of success. It was at the point of my realizing how important trust was to any business endeavor that I adopted a philosophy, which has brought me far. It is this: "A sincere and truthful person in both speech and action attracts to themselves others who appreciate and value integrity."

Having worked with countless individuals including coaches, trainers, management consultants, engineering firms, staffing agencies, human resource consultants, software firms, financial planners, construction firms and executive search firms, I feel comfortable in stating that I understand the skills required for helping companies grow. But skill is not always enough. Having helped an infinite number of independent professionals gain a foothold in the federal and private sector, I have discovered that nothing was as valuable to me as living by a strong code of ethics.

Because of my insistence on building my business based on trust, I have been very fortunate in attracting and being supported by people who provided encouragement, assistance and motivation during various life-altering situations. These special people, that I call my "Guardian Angels," have deeply touched me, enriching my life at every turn. When I needed encouragement during setbacks, they were there. When struggling with critical career decisions, each in their own way acted as important mentors. Not only did they encourage me to be my best self, but they also provided me with the tools that helped in executing dynamic ideas. Couple their mentoring, along with the valuable lessons I learned from my own powerful experiences in the work place, and this book came to life.

My purpose in sharing the information contained within these pages is to be an agent of change. In this fast moving information age, trust is becoming scarce. Based on results, the world no longer beats a path to the door of those who create the best products, but instead reach for those who cultivate trust.

Hence, the theme of this book is primarily focused on the art of integrity and its many inferences. It is in essence a dynamic tool for gaining the full and loyal confidence of business associates. And while I present the ideas for building a foundation of trust, the application of trust and integrity cannot be contrived or feigned, but instead must be inherent within a company's culture. Grounded in sincerity, truthfulness and honesty, I hope the insight and knowledge I have gleaned from my many adventures and experiences will become the missing link for triumphantly selling business ideas.

Robert Moment

1

Introduction

Today we are experiencing a dramatic revolution in the business world, a revolution that involves the way we conduct ourselves in respect to our business associates and potential clients. In fact, it is, a revolution that greatly influences our ability to succeed at selling our services and products.

Because selling is a natural, inherent factor in almost every endeavor, it must be applied with great skill no matter what the service or goods a company is offering. Yet selling has reached a highly competitive art form and is becoming more of a challenge to small companies and organizations than ever before. To maintain a significant market advantage, it is no longer enough to rely solely upon one's professionalism. It is important that added to ordinary measures is the need for forming a bond between business and client that goes above and beyond the norm. It is a bond that we now term *Relationship Marketing*. Despite the methods a company uses to sell its products or services, if a company were to keep up with the times, they would do well to consider Relationship Marketing.

What exactly is Relationship Marketing and what makes it so important to the success of a business? At a basic level, Relationship

Marketing involves trust and must be established early on to ensure confidence between buyer and seller. However, establishing trust is not as simple as it initially sounds. As a point of reference, the trust level within corporate America is currently at its lowest point, given that suspicions are running extremely high, and rising with each passing day.

In today's business world, particularly for those who conduct business via the Internet, the foundation of Relationship Marketing is built upon one single yet vital concept, and that concept is known as *Integrity*. Businesses that hope to survive and thrive in the 21st century must recognize their essential role in establishing honor between all concerned parties. Whether a company is a small Mom and Pop or a large corporation, Relationship Marketing must be incorporated in a business structure to ensure on-going professional connections. The lack of Relationship Marketing appears to be the common denominator among companies that are falling apart or simply not succeeding.

We are no longer interested in dealing with those who demonstrate anything less than their best. Now that we have access to the world via the Internet, countless competitors are more than willing to provide what another company lacks. Consequently, when a company demonstrates trustworthiness, the client perceives this as a quality discovery. As a result, the client is eager to continue working within a relationship that is founded and based on trust.

The bottom line is that clients are avid in their pursuit of relationships with individuals that maintain integrity and good will, or they go elsewhere. The importance of exceptional customer service and other client-pleasing attitudes and approaches are crucial to the success of a business, and have become keys to a company's survival.

However, what is the quality and requirement that builds upon a foundation of trust, and how is one to begin the process of building trust with potential clients? In essence, it begins with an understanding of what trust means. For the purpose of this book, trust is defined as the belief that the seller is operating from a level of honesty and integrity, and leaves no room for suspicion regarding actions or motives. Consequently, turning a business into a trustworthy organization means building upon a level of confidence with each individual client. By carefully eliminating any fear that a client may have regarding a company's motives or ethics, a client is left knowing that the company they're working with has their best interests at heart.

These are the basics of integrity. They are the principles behind and within a company that operates from high standards, and in order to rate high points from the onset of a relationship with the potential client, a foundation of trust must be established. For that purpose, I have coined the term *SCORE* as a method and reminder for scoring high points with clients. SCORE is an acronym for what I believe is at the basis of Relationship Marketing and stands for:

Sincerity

Commitment

Openness

Reliability

Execution

SCORE-ing is a well thought out formula for success that can be applied in any business endeavor. It is a means of establishing a reputation of credibility and integrity with all associates. By forming a trusting relationship with each individual, whether client, business associate or employee, a company has the greatest opportunity for building a thriving, flourishing business. By applying the following principles based on effective Relationship Marketing, a company is on its way to selling its ideas abundantly.

2

Sincerity

"Sincerity is a duty no less plain than important."

—*Knox*

sin·cer·i·ty (sĭn-sĕr´ĭ-tē), *n*. The quality or state of being sincere; honesty of mind or intention; freedom from simulation, hypocrisy, disguise, or false pretense. *(Webster's Revised Unabridged Dictionary,* © *1996, 1998 MICRA, Inc.)*

As I see it, the first and most important qualification, insofar as relationship marketing is concerned, is the quality of sincerity. Whether you are making a presentation to a new client, training your representatives to carry out your message, selling a product online, or offering a much-needed service, sincerity should be at the core of your company ethics.

The dictionary defines sincerity as freedom from hypocrisy, disguise or false pretense, which is at the heart of Relationship Marketing. In the world of business, sincerity is about sharing a product or service you wholeheartedly believe in, conveying your company message with complete enthusiasm, and doing it without pretense. Sincerity is meaning what you say, and being ardent in your approach as you present it. Sincerity requires the action of speaking to each client as if it is the first time you are making a presentation. Simply rehashing the same old lines will more than likely leave the recipient of the *pitch* with a sense of being conned. Instead, selling with sincerity begins with

4

treating each client as an individual, possessing different needs along with a unique personality. Selling with sincerity requires seeing the potential of every situation as new, and fully drawing upon the inherent possibilities.

As we have seen in recent times, no matter how successful or prosperous an individual or business, individuals in charge of a business are often called upon to test their values, particularly when something important is at stake. During those times, any action can later be justified in the name of status, self-esteem, and especially money. And while we may simply be reacting at the time of an incident, and not thinking directly of the consequences, it often becomes easier after the fact to explain away behavior that was not very ethical. In fact, for the majority of us, it's actually surprisingly easy to think of a situation where we may stray from our own personal code of integrity.

So, how do we incorporate and maintain the change required for conducting ourselves, and our professions, with a quality of sincerity, and how can we convince all those on our team of the importance of sincerity in all business matters? Even more significant, how can we instill the importance of sincerity within the very foundation of our company, and never veer from our code of ethics?

The answer lies when we start at the very beginning, which is with the person who is in charge. It is a vital fact that key decisionmakers must first understand the importance of integrity and sincerity in the work place. Before sincerity becomes the way for a company, it must start at the top and then filter down to other members of a team. When owners and managers apply sincerity in all their actions, interactions and communications, they demonstrate to representatives that taking the high road to integrity is the way to go.

At the very core of a company that employs Relationship Marketing, representatives must understand and accept that at every level of responsibility, one says what should be said, and always means what is said. Consider the feeling you experience when you leave an interaction with a potential client knowing that you have given your very best in the situation, and you have done it with sincerity. More than likely, you feel clear of mind and heart. And best of all, you sense that your level of sincerity is felt by all potential customers and existing clients.

To assure that you and your representatives operate from this level of integrity, there is a simple process to follow that becomes the formula for your company. The blueprint for sincerity can be incorporated as follows:

- Choose your desired outcome beforehand

- Have a clear intention in mind

- Determine the process for reaching your outcome

- Evaluate your outcome

- Learn from the experience

1) Choose Your Desired Outcome

To know where you are headed, you must choose a clear direction for your path. After all, if you don't know where you're going, how will you get there? In other words, if you wish to incorporate the Relationship Marketing theory into your company ethics, you must first recognize what type of outcome you are hoping to achieve. Simply stated, you have to start by knowing your desired outcome beforehand. Once you understand your purpose, you can take appropriate steps that lead in the direction of your goal. Certainly, there are many ways in which a particular goal can be attain, but when applying the SCORE method, the roadmap is very clear and you never get lost.

2) Have a Clear Intention

Individuals who apply relationship marketing utilize the power of intention to envision their goals. Reaping the fruits of your labor is, of course, a clear intention and certainly a legitimate purpose, but for the sake of developing trust and sincerity within an organization, we are moving beyond mere financial gain. A more elevated intention, and one that is less self-serving, will be the guiding force that propels you in the right direction. This intention is to be of service, and thus, ensure that you are helping your client.

3) Discover the process for reaching your outcome

The next time you move forward, ask yourself if you explored all viable options for reaching your outcome. Were you honest and sincere in your motivations? Were you as eager to see the client succeed as you were to make the sale? Did you apply a method that felt good? An intention creates a very strong and qualifying aspect of any enterprise. Once you have reached the outcome desired, reason it through carefully so that you are certain of your method. Perhaps another approach might be even better. When a similar situation appears, you'll be in a position to define your intention, and better able to outline your process.

4) Evaluate the Outcome

Evaluate your outcome with regard to the lengths taken in order to reach your outcome. Are you pleased with the methods you used? Do you feel that the client was as pleased with your strategy as you were with the outcome? Was it a win/win for everyone? When all sides of an interaction feel the value of the outcome, you know that you have applied sincerity as a part of relationship marketing. The motivation that compels others to conduct business with you over others comes from your intention of genuine and sincere service.

5) Learn from the experience

Finally, use the entire process as a learning tool, so that you may perfect future interactions. Next time apply even more sincerity and authenticity with regard to your clients. Your ultimate desire should be to reach the appropriate outcome in the right way for all concerned. If you sincerely want to apply *Relationship Marketing*, always say what you mean and mean what you say. Have confidence in what you're conveying, so the other party feels a sense of trust. An intention that has an underlying message of unquestionable authenticity, coupled with a desire to help others will take you very far. That quality will immediately draw others to take action.

Keep in mind that sincerity is a blatantly clear attribute. In reverse, almost anyone will be put off by its opposite. Because sincerity is ultimately a team effort, as much as it is an individual effort, it is imperative that sincerity comes across in all transactions. The best way to achieve this is to work towards having every member of a team believing in what they do. If a member of your team believes in the company products or services, they won't have any trouble being sincere.

As the leader of your company, it is important that you make every effort to promote sincerity by making certain each team member knows his or her value to the team. In truth, each team player's opinion is beneficial, whatever their role in the company. When team members know they are a part of something larger than they are, they become convinced of their worth. In turn, they believe in what they do. When representatives believe in what they do, then they give their all—which leads to greater client trust, satisfaction and greater success.

3

Commitment

"Unless commitment is made, there are only promises and hopes...but no plans."

—*Peter Drucker*

com·mit·ment (kə-mĭt′mənt), *n.* The state of being bound emotionally or intellectually to a course of action or to another person or persons. *(The American Heritage® Dictionary of the English Language, Fourth Edition Copyright © 2000 by Houghton Mifflin Company)*

Having a commitment to your goals is a remarkable characteristic and brings with it an exceptional amount of power. However, we are often confused by what it means to sell with commitment and don't understand exactly what it implies in the business world. As an aspect of Relationship Marketing, commitment selling is essential to your company's success and should be high on your list of achievements.

With your intention of sincerity already in place, the next step in gearing up a Relationship Marketing company is establishing a commitment to yourself, your representatives and to your clients. Johann Wolfgang Von Goethe put it perfectly when he stated, "Until one is committed, there is hesitancy, the chance to draw back, always ineffectiveness. Concerning all acts of initiative and creation, there is one elementary truth, the ignorance of which kills countless ideas and splendid plans: that the moment one definitely commits oneself, and then providence moves too. All sorts of things occur to help one that would never otherwise have occurred. A whole stream of events issues from the decision, raising in one's favor all manner of unforeseen incidents, meetings and material assistance that no man could have dreamed would have come his way. Whatever you can do or dream you can, begin it. Boldness has genius, power and magic in it. Begin it now."

In other words, to sell with commitment means we start by making a commitment to ourselves. When the guiding principles of a company are reflected in the attitudes of the owner, manager, or supervisor's core values, it is then that a framework of commitment prevails. In addition, when an intention of commitment is completely installed in a company's culture, it becomes an attitude that operates without notice. Consequently, when company representatives operate from a level of commitment, they aren't conscious of the fact that they are turning what was once considered *selling* into a natural, yet very profitable conversation.

The aspect of selling with commitment at first may seem obscure, but with further exploration, its importance and significance becomes clear. Having a commitment to ethical business conduct is critical to the continued success of any company, and when the right standards are in place, a representative of a Relationship Marketing company will have fully integrated the value of commitment, naturally assuming the role of integrity selling.

Once the seller believes in his or her product, they sell with a desire to be of service. Although there is a subtle difference between the sellers who believes in his or her product wholeheartedly compared to those who sell merely to make a living, the client senses the underlying commitment and appreciates the naturalness of the seller's presentation. Selling with commitment can be summed up in simple terms. No matter how tough a situation may be, the seller sticks to his or her level of commitment, whether things go right or not. That is being committed.

A representative, who understands the quality of commitment and lives it, transports a message that leaves the client feeling confidence in the seller's product or service. The committed seller is ready, willing and always unwavering in doing whatever it takes to maintain the principles of integrity. Rest assured, once you make a commitment to your principles you will be challenged by external pressures, but once a commitment is made nothing sways the representative who sells with sincerity and commitment.

When selling with commitment, there is no *hard sell*, and conversation flows easily between buyer and seller. Sincerity is behind all actions, which allows the client to maintain some semblance of choice. Rather than feeling forced into an uncomfortable situation, the buyer soon realizes it is safe to learn more about a product that was previously not known. This type of selling leads to the deeper understanding and psychology behind sales. Selling with commitment is selling in a way where all parties win. The formula for selling with commitment is as follows:

- Selling with Commitment Requires Integrity Selling

- Selling with Commitment is a Way of Life

- Selling with Commitment Requires Listening

- Selling with Commitment Requires Confronting Negative Responses

- Selling with Commitment Requires a Conversational Sales Style

1) Selling with Commitment Requires Integrity Selling

Developing a commitment towards integrity selling is a little different from simply committing to selling your product, and takes a bit of explanation. When encouraging representatives towards commitment selling, you are qualifying them to sell with integrity. Basically, you are encouraging your representatives to move towards a greater understanding of a client's needs. It will require spending extra time with your representatives, helping them gain insight into what the client needs by way of simple, honest dedication. To succeed at reaching this type of selling, you should hire representatives very carefully, making certain they uphold the same values of integrity you wish to convey throughout all aspects of your business.

2) Selling with Commitment is a Way of Life

Selling with commitment is actually a way of life. It begins with the representative knowing that his or her product has value and is worth the client's time and money. The representative takes whatever time is necessary for explaining honestly and clearly, what he or she has to offer. Selling with commitment is based on character more than it is on actual skill development. Nevertheless, there are certain skills that can be developed, and which greatly improve upon the way one sells. The grasping of these skills is quite simple; however, the application takes a great deal of commitment.

3) Selling with Commitment Requires Listening

The first ingredient when selling with commitment is a matter of listening. In fact, 70% of all selling requires listening. Listening begins by asking probing, but necessary questions that help the seller understand the client's needs. Once the seller has asked the question, he or she listens carefully without interruption as to what the potential buyer has to say. Consequently, if the seller asks quality questions and listens intently to the response, channels of communication open up that allow the client to express their true needs. In that way, the seller is better able to address the client's specific circumstances. Influential questions frequently begin with, "Is there any reason that...?" When a question is posed in that manner, it's difficult for the other person to just say *no*.

4) Selling with Commitment Requires Confronting Negative Responses

Many potential clients have become somewhat jaded towards salespeople and often come up with reasons for saying no. Nevertheless, saying no isn't always a bad thing. In fact, it provides an opportunity for allowing the potential client to share their reasons for being hesitant. The less resistance you have to their attitude, the easier it will be to turn the situation into something more productive. Turning a *no* response into a potential *yes* response isn't difficult and is one of the best ways to demonstrate your commitment to integrity.

5) Selling with Commitment Requires Brevity in Your Communication

Remember that no one is interested in hearing a lecture or a long canned presentation, so keeping your delivery brief is vital to your sales communication. Begin by opening with a statement that is soft such as, "Perhaps I may assist you in making a more informed decision?" Another question could be, "May I offer you some quick reasons as to why I believe you would benefit from the product or service in question?" These types of questions open the door to easy conversation and usually lead to providing more information. Remember that the door opener is always brief and to the point.

6) Selling with Commitment Requires a Conversational Sales Style

Developing a *conversational* sales style will take a bit of effort, since most of us have been trained to push hard to make the sale. Yet with a relaxed conversational sales style, you will quickly discover that clients are more open and receptive to the comfortable approach compared to the old style sales pitch. This type of style communicates the appreciation you have for your product or service. When there is no need to exaggerate or mislead, you gain a new perspective for what you are selling. You simply abandon the attitude of trying to sell, and instead, adopt the approach of committed selling to those who need and want your products.

These value-focused, integrity-committed sales approaches, build upon success and help focus on the needs of the client. When the buyer senses that the sales person is not only interested in making a sale, but that the salesperson is above all interested in hearing the clients needs and that the product is suited to the client's requirements, you have in place a commitment to integrity selling. This aspect of Relationship Marketing often develops long-term business commitments.

Your goal is to make sure that the client feels comfortable so that they become long-term repeat clients. Although a commitment to integrity selling requires time to evolve and grow as it continuously changes, the advantage of using this method frees up a great deal of employee potential. In actuality, it enables everyone to use untapped skills that enhance the client's experience. Furthermore, when representatives are committed to sharing information that best suits the client's needs, clients are in a better mode to hear more about your company, its products and services. For commitment selling to work, there must be a great deal of desire and dedication from all parties involved in your organization. With a full commitment from everyone, you can and will create, an organization known for integrity.

4

Openness

○ ○

"She did not talk to people as if they were strange hard shells she had to crack open to get inside. She talked as if she were already in the shell. In their very shell."

—*Marita Bonner*

o·pen·ness (ō´pən-něs), n. characterized by an attitude of ready accessibility especially about one's actions or purposes; not secretive *(WordNet ® 1.6, © 1997 Princeton University)*

We have explored sincerity and commitment selling and now have the beginning of a strong Relationship Marketing Company. The next step in the SCORE program is creating an atmosphere of openness and disclosure both for your representatives and your clients. Because openness suggests more than just sincerity with your clients, it is our belief that openness extends even further as it reflects on how your organization operates from within. For the sake of clarity, achieving a sincere attitude of openness must first start in your business environment, where it affects your representatives.

Openness with Your Representatives

It is in an environment that is open and receptive that everyone grows and flourishes. Instead of an atmosphere that is confusing, hidden or secretive, an open environment encourages everyone to speak freely.

The more freedom you provide your representatives, the more respected they feel. It naturally follows that if your representatives feel respected and safe, they act in the same manner towards clients.

To begin the process of having an open environment, we start by removing fear and doubt in your company environment, which allows representatives to work without behavioral constraints. This is not to imply that anyone can do anything they please, for that would make no sense, but roadblocks to development are formed through fear and doubt and keep representatives from giving their best.

Two of the most common roadblocks to success are rejection and fear of failure. In an organization where Relationship Marketing is at the basis of company policies, all fears are openly discussed. Those who work in a very structured, closed environment may feel rejected if their ideas are not taken seriously or if a client rejects their sales presentation. If a representative believes that their input is of no consequence, they feel unworthy, unwanted and not valued. It can then take a very long time for a person to recover from workplace rejection.

The strong leader of a Relationship Marketing company does not inhibit an individual by squashing his or her ideas or rejecting them entirely, but instead, encourages them to share their ideas. Acceptance leads to confidence, which in turn affects client relationships. When representatives view themselves positively, new ideas evolve and problems soon disappear.

Because success is very closely related to one's reaction to inevitable failures, and since no one gets through life without experiencing some form of failure, it's up to the leader of an organization to create an environment where people aren't afraid to fail. If representatives display fear and doubt both in themselves and their products, it is reflected back through a lack of trust from clients. Instead of being ruled by the fear of failure, the wise employer encourages representatives to express their fears, openly facing them, which in turn encourages them to let the fear of failure go.

In a SCORE based environment, representatives are not punished for making mistakes or for being afraid, but are instead inspired to strive for excellence. By helping representatives know who they are, what they are capable of achieving, and their potential value to the company, you are helping to create representatives who understand Relationship Marketing.

Since people do not hand over their money to just anyone, but instead buy from those they trust, through openness your representatives learn how to demonstrate a high level of trust. In an environment founded on openness, representatives are comfortable expressing themselves. This in turn translates to expressing openly to clients. In that way, your company establishes important rapport that will not be broken.

Once representatives feel comfortable with the open mode of operation, they carry this same attitude out into their sales presentations, not fearing rejection or failure, but better able to convince clients of their ability to meet their needs. Rejection from a client no longer has the hold on a representative that it previously held.

Openness with Your Clients

Now that your representatives feel safe and open in their work environment, they are in a better position to show clients what your company can do for them. Building long-term relationships based on trust means establishing openness that puts your clients at ease. When clients are at ease, you are in an ideal situation to succeed. When an underlying connectivity continues to be the constant in a Relationship Marketing environment, the company continues to grow and move forward.

It is at this point that we stress the importance of making all relevant information about your products and services very clear to the client. Based on this high level of disclosure, it is your job to make sure you establish the following:

- A clear expression of the terms and conditions regarding any trans-actions within your business—whether in a physical store or online.

- Return policies

- The number of days it will take to fulfill an order

- The method of delivery used

- Rain check policies—or alternatives

- Payment options

- Processing policies (such as customer will not be billed until his or her item has been shipped)

- Describing the item (new or used, color, brand, overall description)

- Warranty definitions

- Service and support availability related to the item

- Service options

As you can see, it should be your overall goal to make it clear that you are what you seem to be—especially if you're operating an online business. When a client visits a physical store, he or she can see the items being sold, plus they can hold and purchase the items. But selling by way of the Internet, a person can pretend to sell anything, yet not be an actual company. To display openness and integrity to your clients, four important components must be included:

- The first is compliance with all of the stated business practices regard-ing each and every transaction that occurs within your company

- Second is the ability to perform satisfactory follow ups when needed; for example, dealing with client questions or complaints immediately

- Third is the monitoring of all transactions so that updates and corrections can be made quickly—especially in a case of non-compliance

- Fourth is showing that management cares and is always willing to conduct trustworthy transactions.

Openness Regarding Online Stores

Because online privacy is an extremely relevant issue in today's business world, clients need to know that if they choose to enter information on your web site; all relevant information provided will be safe.

To that end, your company should openly demonstrate the following provisions:

- You will do everything in your power to prevent the transmission of personal information by way of the Internet to unintended parties

- You will make sure to prevent outside access

- You will always take steps to prevent the inappropriate use of personal information by your own representatives

- You will prevent the unauthorized permission of modifying the personal files of clients (most commonly involving the use of "cookies")

Any company making a statement of integrity, whether operated by way of a physical store or an online presence, should display the aforementioned items as the bare minimum concerning their openness with clients.

If the above issues are violated, you may also wish to include additional reimbursement policies. Additionally, if the client chooses to remain anonymous, you will respect their privacy by not sharing information. It is your role as the leader of your company to use openness as a means of conveying the message that your company is trustworthy. Openness demonstrates that you have nothing to hide. If clients inquire, they should be able to ascertain and understand everything about your company.

5

Reliability

"The only lifelong, reliable motivations are those that come from within, and one of the strongest of those is the joy and pride that grow from knowing that you've just done something as well as you can do it."

—*Lloyd Dobens and Clare Crawford-Mason,*
Thinking About Quality

re·li·a·ble (rĭ-lī'ə-bəl), adj. Capable of being relied on; dependable (*The American Heritage® Dictionary of the English Language, Fourth Edition Copyright © 2000 by Houghton Mifflin Company*)

Reliability is the foundation on which you build a level of trust with clients. When you break it down to its most basic level, selling with reliability means helping clients make important purchasing decisions. Selling, when done with a high factor of integrity, is more of a people business than a product business. Therefore, your time, energy and effort primarily should focus on the people, and not as much on the product. No matter how exceptional or extraordinary your product, a product alone never builds a business of integrity.

To develop a business that is reliable in the eyes of the consumer, an organization must be grounded in the concept of Relationship Marketing, which incorporates representatives that identify with the values of the business. In other words, those you hire should know why your business exists; what its intentions are; and what type of mark you intend to leave. For clients to return repeatedly, the overall theme of a company that operates from reliability should be one that conveys sincerity, commitment, openness and reliability.

Although potential clients often have resistance to sales people, in actuality, people love to buy, especially if they see the advantage of the product. The problem with selling often stems from years of selling without integrity. In the new paradigm of Relationship Marketing, the more powerful way of selling is by understanding the needs and motives of the client first, seeing beneath the surface of why people buy. The person who sells with reliability works hard initially at knowing why people buy rather than how to sell and always tries to understand the client. For potential clients to have an interest in your product or service, they must sense that your level of reliability is superior.

Reliability in the marketplace covers a wide range of territory, and includes more than how you sell. It also should embrace moral and ethical issues as well. How you conduct your business is crucial at every level.

Before addressing the reliability of moral and ethical issues, let's start with several critical points that should be considered when initially dealing with clients.

Acting Reliably in Regard to Your Clients:

1. When a company has a foundation of reliability, it has a solid understanding of the buying motives of its clients. Essentially, you and your representatives must explore and understand the reasons your clients buy; what their needs are and how you can help them achieve their goals. In essence, it is about understanding a client's motivation.

2. When a company bases its reputation on reliability, it builds quality rapport with both established clients and potential clients. In other words, you and your representatives get to know your clients

as people, not as a means of persuading them, but as a means of being of service.

3. When a company is based on reliability, it takes the time and patience to effectively explain why a potential client should make a purchase through your company. No matter how many questions are asked or how long it takes the client to decide, it should make no difference to your representatives.

4. When a company is based on reliability, it has a clear concept of what questions should be asked, what things should be said and certainly what type of conduct to apply in order to effectively sell its products. Winning a client's trust comes from repeated positive experiences. Consistent actions are what a client perceives as reliable.

5. When a company is based on reliability, referrals easily turn into clients. By demonstrating all the important aspects of Relationship Marketing, including integrity, sincerity, reliability and openness, others learn of your credibility through word of mouth and are eager to establish a working relationship with you.

6. When a company is based on reliability, it is committed to clear, professional actions, which means having no agenda, exceeding client expectations and delivering a quality product or service on time. Basically, the rule should be under promise, but over deliver.

7. When a company is based on reliability, it follows-up activities and carefully monitors transactions. Follow-up can be a simple phone call or even sending a brief note. Follow-up often on how things are going for your client and drop personalized thank you notes occasionally to let them know you are thinking of them. The phrase thank you can never be said often enough, especially when you are an integrity-based company

It is highly recommended that these points be practiced consistently. In addition, it should also be made clear to your clients that these points are always addressed and practiced.

Should a client find that a particular point isn't handled in an appropriate manner, they should feel comfortable enough to approach you.

The best way to evaluate your company's reliability is by going through each of the above points, seriously considering one key point at a time. Place a mark next to any point where you believe your company may be lacking. And don't be surprised if you have a mark next to each point, since almost every company can use a bit of improvement! Never hesitate to be *tough* in your evaluation of your company, since improvements only mean the enhancement of your business.

Corruption or Political Instability

Earlier, there was brief mention of moral and ethical issues that confront most companies. The subject warrants further investigation.

Because reliability and trust are at the foundation of integrity, operating a Relationship Marketing company requires a serious defense against corruption and political instability. An organization that operates from reliability is completely free from any aspect of corruption with no exceptions. Corruption covers more than just stealing money, it is also a matter of stealing trust, in addition to being morally and economically damaging.

There is a very fine line dividing actions with integrity from actions that are corrupt. However, to remain a reliable company, it is important that clear definitions of what is acceptable and not acceptable should be well defined, leaving nothing left to interpretation. It takes only one single transgression to compromise the integrity of a company; one must be careful about losing the sense of reliability that has taken so long to form. Common definitions of breaches of integrity follow:

1) Bribes

Bribes occur when a payment is made to sway the decision of a representative of the company. Often bribes are made so that the representative will do something that is out of alignment with the integrity of the company, or they are asked to omit something that should have been performed under the rules or policies, which govern the transaction. While it is wrong for someone to offer a bribe, it is infinitely worse for the integrity of your company if the bribe is accepted.

2) Gratuities

While there are certain instances or types of employment where gratuities are acceptable, such as tipping a waitress, hairdresser or the like, if gifts, favors, discounts, entertainment, hospitality, loans, or other items of monetary value are given to sway favor, reliability and integrity are at risk. Keep in mind that there are items to which this breach of integrity does not apply. Sharing inexpensive pens, mugs, mouse pads, or possibly the modest provision of food and refreshments, such as soft drinks, coffee, and donuts are acceptable. A meal in some circumstances is agreeable if you are visiting a client's location and resort to a restaurant or cafeteria for a meeting. Naturally, discretion and common sense are the keys to assuring that your reliability is not compromised through impropriety.

3) Offering Employment

It is acceptable in many circumstances to offer a person employment, however, it cannot be in exchange for certain actions, nor can it be to receive inside information about another company. You should only offer employment if you sincerely believe that the person has something valuable to bring to your team, and, in addition, their values fit in with your level of integrity.

4) Kickbacks

Kickbacks are any monies, fees, commissions, or gifts given by either a subcontractor or a supplier to the contractor, as a means of obtaining favorable treatment. To maintain integrity in your business, you should prohibit kickbacks of all kinds and should be clear at the onset of hiring representatives as to your strict policy against kickbacks.

5) Independent Pricing

A standard price, price structure, or price estimate guide should be established within your company so that everyone receives the same fair treatment. Reliability regarding pricing is a very large issue among businesses and their clients. To assure clients that they are valuable to you, they should be treated fairly. If a client should discover that they are not receiving equal treatment, your relationship with the client will be threatened.

6) Record Maintenance

Keeping superior records means that you stay on top of the activities and actions of your company at all times. Clients are in a better position to build on a foundation of trust when they know that you can call up or track any action whenever it is requested. If you cannot confirm a shipment, or verify any other type of transaction, your client may feel as though they are dealing with an unreliable company.

7) Falsification of Records

Falsifying records is closely related to the aforementioned *record maintenance* issue. Falsifying or destroying records with the intention of hiding non-compliance, or attempting to make it appear as though compliance is being upheld, means you cannot be relied upon for honesty. This includes records that relate to the origin of your products and issues regarding employment. A reliable company not only maintains truthful employment records, but also states honestly where goods originated. If there is inconsistency and dishonesty, there is no integrity.

8) Product Integrity

Your clients should know they are getting what they pay for, plus they are getting what's expected. Your products should be clearly and accurately labeled, and should not be substituted with shoddy parts or reduced performance. The only exception would be if a product clearly states that there is an issue of "irregularity." Making sure to establish that your product is consistently worth the money spent is an extremely critical part of demonstrating reliability to your clients. If you should fail, more than likely, your clients will go elsewhere immediately.

Go over each point of your policies and procedures meticulously, making certain that you are demonstrating the utmost of integrity to your clients. Consideration and adherence to all of the above points as they apply to your company are vital to your client and to your business. Demonstrating that you are reliable conveys the message that you can be trusted. Should you waver or fall short on any level, your reliability will be shaken, and your integrity will be in question.

6

Execution

"Show up on time, with a plan, a commitment to carry it out, and then execute it."

—*Harvey Mackay*

ex'e-cute (ek'si-kyut'), *v.* Do, perform; to carry out fully; put completely into effect. To do what is provided or required; to make or produce by carrying out a design. (*Webster's Revised Unabridged Dictionary,* © *1996, 1998 MICRA, Inc*)

As you can see by the above definition, the execution of SCORE is by far one of the most critical steps for putting forth this new strategy. Executing your plan means putting into action a new paradigm focused on a sincere, committed, open, reliable strategy, wherein you, your team and your clients are totally in alignment. To complete and fulfill the process, you must be able to communicate your ideas effectively to all concerned parties. Transmitting your ideas powerfully means executing your strategy with every person you encounter.

While dynamic plans and new strategies bring excitement, enthusiasm and encouragement to the entrepreneur, they have no real effect if the right type of execution is lacking. No matter how fabulous your strategy or intentions, unless everything you have planned is put into action, it will be useless to your company. Plain and simple, the way you execute the SCORE method can mean the difference between a mediocre company and one that stands above the crowd.

Although the SCORE concept has been well thought out and applied in numerous environments, many people fall short when it comes to the execution phase. The reason being is that all aspects of Relationship Marketing must be applied consistently, conscientiously and diligently for it to work effectively. In addition, each aspect must be monitored carefully or it gives way to defeat.

It is at the point of execution that everyone associated with your organization becomes greatly empowered; however, it is up to you to assure that everyone is clear on the entire Relationship Marketing theory. It is during this phase that each team member begins to focus both on the inner workings of the company, as well as the outer. It is also usually at this stage that everyone starts to feel the stretch as they apply and execute a new way of conducting business.

To avoid failing at this stage of the game, start your action plan by examining and analyzing all business situations and goals prior to executing the SCORE strategy. Be sure that you have focused in on the areas that appear to be the most deficient and then set priorities. The best way to achieve that is by identifying your highest priorities, addressing all the substantial aspects of your business. Although the various phases of SCORE are all important, they don't necessarily have to be applied in any special order. As long as you have a clear plan in place, SCORE will come together effectively if you follow it carefully.

As you go through your priorities, focus on the specific issues that you feel certain will bring the fastest and greatest results. In support of your efforts, be open and willing to make adjustments and changes, as they seem evident. And be willing to draw upon ideas and information from other team members, making sure everyone is in agreement.

With sincerity, commitment, openness and reliability in place, it will not be difficult to translate the meaning and value of SCORE to your team members. However, it is critical that each member of your company is clear as to their role in executing the goals of your company. The SCORE strategy is simple, and once put into practice, will reap obvious results, but must be applied by everyone involved.

Many companies use measures that help test the execution results of the SCORE strategy. For example, if your goal was to adjust a communication problem you would keep track as to any negative recurrences, making sure you are getting to the root cause of the problem. One way to measure results, thereby gaining a clear picture of where your team is at with SCORE, would be by having leadership meetings once a month. It is during those meetings that problems are discussed and individuals openly support each other in handling specific challenges. Essentially, your new plan must be reviewed periodically to bring about positive change.

To build upon the strategy you are eager to implement, there are some highly recommended steps and stages that should be included. Consider the following:

1. Clearly establish all key elements, procedures, and methods that will be followed by you, your company, and all its representatives. Make certain that evaluations are objective and fair to all parties involved.

2. Reduce opportunities for violations of integrity by using unmistakable procedures based upon the criteria discussed in previous chapters.

3. Protect your integrity by safeguarding against any corrupt practices through written or verbal contracts. Include compulsory conditions and regulations concerning the roles of each partner or representative in the execution of the project.

4. When working with other companies make certain that you are capable of protecting their high ethical standards and codes of conduct. In other words, demonstrate that you practice integrity not only within your own company, but also in connection to your external relations as well.

5. When you're searching for potential clients, seek out those that have similar high ethical standards to the ones you practice within your own company. Just as a company can tell that you are a Relationship Marketing Company, you'll be able to evaluate another by the same criteria.

6. Your commitment to integrity should be reflected clearly in your mission statement, policies and procedures; the representatives of your company, your clients, and other businesses must clearly understand the importance you place on integrity.

7. As you continue to develop and establish your business integrity within your own company, do whatever is necessary to unfailingly assure that it is applied as needed at all levels, including management, staff and training programs.

8. Keep yourself and your business current and up to date in regard to local laws and regulations that confront corrupt practices; breaches in these laws to the proper legal enforcement authorities should be reported.

9. Determine very clearly at the onset that team members understand the consequences of violating any rule or policy of integrity and ethics.

10. Take prompt disciplinary action against any team member within your company if it has been discovered they have violated any of your rules or policies of integrity. These disciplinary actions should be swift, legal, and confidential.

11. In support of your efforts, take part in local or national organizations whose goals curb or penalize corrupt practices in businesses.

Executing your integrity strategy favorably both to your representatives and to your clients is a challenge, but certainly one worthy of your efforts. Applying all the principles of SCORE is not a quick process but it will open up an infinite number of opportunities, thereby assisting you in maximizing the full potential of your business. You simply decide exactly what your company stands for, how it will accomplish its goals and how you will demonstrate your high level of integrity to potential and established clients, and before you know it, SCORE will have taken the lead.

A few points to remember

- Before you engage your strategy, have it well charted out.

- Understand what integrity means to you before you apply it.

- Make sure that the rest of your staff and team members understand integrity based on your terms.

- Be prepared to conduct training session at various levels

- SCORE should be implemented in all aspects of your company including customer service, sales strategies and product information.

Initially, executing the SCORE strategy may seem overwhelming, but let me assure you that you are already further into the process than you realize. You were drawn to this type of material, which implies that you already operate from a level of integrity. Your desire to run a full-fledged Relationship Marketing company can only be an added bonus for your organization. Moreover, once the plan is in place, it is perpetual.

Executing your new integrity strategy is of course an ongoing process. And if you start out right, it will continue to get better. The path of improvement becomes easier and easier until it is simply a natural part of the way you run your business.

7

Conclusion

o o o o o o o o o o o o o o o o o o o o o o o o o o o o o o o o
"Integrity without knowledge is weak and useless, and knowledge without integrity is dangerous and dreadful."

—*Samuel Johnson (1709–1784)*

In truth, achieving SCORE should be about who you are as an individual as well as a business owner and not so much about building a business and prospering. To SCORE big, you should be making your priorities more about relationships with clients, partners, representatives, and vendors and the rest follows.

These initiatives are not one-time actions, but must be enforced for the lifetime of a company. As mentioned previously, selling is a natural, inherent factor in almost every endeavor, but to sell with integrity requires practicing Relationship Marketing. In other words, we should be forming bonds that bring us together rather than tearing us apart. Integrity in the work place should be typical and not the unusual.

We must begin taking responsibility for our actions, demonstrating that we can be both trusted and relied upon. We simply cannot wait or even expect governments to impose regulations upon companies, compelling us to display a strong sense of integrity. Besides, it wouldn't work. What must be done is that we ourselves take on the responsibility of integrity by applying the SCORE concept.

Integrity is a matter of values, mores, and the personal integrity of each member of a team. Achieving SCORE integrity is aligning with principles, all of which have tremendous earning and ethical potential.

The rewards of a SCORE company will take many forms including stronger relationships, better and more business, and happier individuals. You will feel secure each time you make a sale, beginning a chain of *word of mouth clients*, the best kind of promotion a business can hope to achieve. Moreover, you will be rewarded with a sense of knowing that you are doing your best, assisting valued clients in making the right decisions that meet their needs and not just yours. The satisfaction of knowing that you are operating from a high level of integrity brings with it a deep sense of gratification and accomplishment.

SCORE integrity maintains the following parameters

1. Avoids misunderstandings in regard to violations of a company's values of integrity by never assuming anything; all integrity policies and agreements must be set forth clearly and explicitly early on, so that nothing is left to interpretation.

2. A genuine SCORE commitment requires that all members of a team must adopt the company's code of ethics and integrity as his or her own; a violation of integrity then becomes everyone's issue.

3. Laws, rules, and regulations that have already been set must be followed strictly; personal choice should not take precedence when it concerns business matters.

4. Mores should define the shared understanding within a company in respect to what is correct, good, and worthy.

5. The professional integrity within your company must become the overall integrity of your business.

Authentic integrity is not simply a matter of company policy, or a few representatives practicing these policies, but rather is a matter of unity and wholeness within a business. To succeed, your company must be able to depend upon itself for the practice and enforcement of words and actions of integrity throughout the company.

Any abandonment of integrity that may occur should not be treated laxly, nor should it be excused with simple conversation. Any violation of integrity, whether it is intentional insincerity, deceitfulness, or some other lack of integrity, should have consequences that are clearly defined and outlined prior to the event occurring. If a representative cannot or will not comply with the standard of integrity you've set for your company, they should not be in your company.

Integrity, therefore, is not a simple matter of valuing order or being intolerant of disobedience. Promoting integrity also requires delving into dissent if it occurs. Rather than running for cover when an issue of disagreement or conflict occurs, it must be explored.

There are some very strong examples of individuals with integrity, namely Mahatma Gandhi, Mother Teresa, and Jesus Christ to name a few, who demonstrated the intensity of their convictions, but through magnificent acts of civil disobedience. This is not to say that disruption and inconvenience should be encouraged, but it should not be ignored.

A business is wise to promote integrity through explicit rules in addition to values that are genuinely shared by members of your organization. However, complaints from clients, representatives and other businesses should be taken seriously. The issues must be resolved in a way as to guarantee they won't recur in the future. You know it is resolved when an overall improvement is achieved.

*Integrity is available to anyone who is willing to practice it
with awareness and discipline.*

To SCORE with integrity, we must act with *Sincerity, Commitment, Openness* and *Reliability* to ourselves and to others. We must establish and maintain integrity by being honest with others about what we stand for and demonstrating that we are reliable. We must then *Execute* these actions in a way that is appealing to everyone involved.

Creating an organization with *whole* business integrity comes about when personal integrity and business integrity feed off each other perpetuating integrity at every level within an entire company. When your particular code of integrity is clearly outlined, properly enforced and repeatedly acknowledged, personal integrity builds within each individual.

In essence, a business with integrity follows basic disciplines

1. A business operating from a high state of integrity always does what it says it will do, consequently, it is a trusted business

2. A business operating from a high state of integrity guides its representatives towards making ethical business decisions

3. A business operating from a high state of integrity does the right thing without having to think about it

4. A business operating from a high state of integrity does the right thing

5. A business operating from a high state of integrity takes responsibility for its actions

6. A business operating from a high state of integrity maintains its own weight

7. A business operating from a high state of integrity thinks holistically (whole, entire, complete)

8. A business operating from a high state of integrity recommits and reaffirms their commitment to operating with integrity every year.

9. A business operating from a high state of integrity respects others

10. A business operating from a high state of integrity reflects often on its actions so that it learns from the past

11. A business operating from a high state of integrity clearly defines rules, roles, and values

The better the relations you have with clients, representatives, and partners, the better your company performance will be. As a true leader, you must earn the trust of all involved, carefully examining opinions in so far as business decisions, concerns, matters and issues. When you take care of other people, other people take care of you. Understanding, knowledge, and care will lead you down the path of integrity, to the place where your business can truly SCORE!

It is only through the commitment of SCORE that the world of business will change for the better. I believe that these changes can occur if we unite as professionals. If everyone applied these principles, than the true meaning of integrity will emerge strong in Corporate America.

It is my sincerest hope that through the message of SCORE, you can start on a new journey of integrity, making a difference in your own individual business, helping to transform the business world one company at a time. The future of business is in our hands and working together can and will make the difference. Only through executing the strategy of SCORE will we find companies changing for the better. Haphazard application won't work, but a full commitment to ALL the principles will change the course and direction of the business world. Let's put it to work and see amazing results!

I wish you the best in your new adventure. Please feel free to write me and share your experiences using the SCORE method and take a moment to visit my web site at www.sellintegrity where you will learn more about selling with integrity.

About the Author

Robert Moment

As a highly knowledgeable businessman with very strong work ethics, Robert Moment clearly understands the need for executing integrity in the business world and works hard at conveying his message to the masses. Having proven himself as an exceptionally ethical professional, Robert has earned a reputation as a sought after consultant who flourishes in the business environment.

Founder of **The Moment Group**, Robert works closely with small business owners, revealing the often-challenging, yet mysterious, secrets of winning federal contracts. With nearly two decades of experience to his credit, Mr. Moment displays an exceptional grasp on the art of integrity and is recognized for his astute business insight and high customer satisfaction.

You can learn more about Robert Moment by visiting www. sellintegrity.com where you will discover ideas about selling with integrity.

0-595-31833-9